27th International Conference on Computational Linguistics (COLING 2018)

Tutorial Abstracts

Santa Fe, New Mexico, USA
20 – 26 August 2018

ISBN: 978-1-5108-6906-6

Printed from e-media with permission by:

Curran Associates, Inc.
57 Morehouse Lane
Red Hook, NY 12571

Some format issues inherent in the e-media version may also appear in this print version.

Printed by Curran Associates, Inc. (2018)

Association for Computational Linguistics
209 N. Eighth Street
Stroudsburg, Pennsylvania 18360

Phone: 1-570-476-8006
Fax: 1-570-476-0860

acl@aclweb.org

Additional copies of this publication are available from:

Curran Associates, Inc.
57 Morehouse Lane
Red Hook, NY 12571 USA
Phone: 845-758-0400
Fax: 845-758-2633
Email: curran@proceedings.com
Web: www.proceedings.com

COLING 2018

The 27th International Conference on Computational Linguistics

Proceedings of Tutorial Abstracts

August 20th, 2018
Santa Fe, New Mexico, USA

This volume contains the abstracts of the COLING 2018 tutorials. This year we had a joint call-for-tutorials, coordinated with the tutorial co-chairs for ACL, NAACL, and EMNLP. We received 49 submissions to the joint call, making the selection highly competitive. Through a process that involved the nine co-chairs placing bids on their preferred tutorials, COLING chose to host six tutorials covering a range of core problems and exciting developments in computational linguistics and natural language processing. These tutorials, each of 3 hours, will be held on Monday 20th of August.

This is an exciting time for our field, and we hope that you will enjoy the tutorials that are on offer for COLING 2018 in Santa Fé, New Mexico.

COLING 2018 Tutorial Chairs
Donia Scott
Marilyn Walker
Pascale Fung

Table of Contents

NLP for Conversations

Gabriel Murray
UFV
Canada
gabriel.murray@ufv.ca

Shafiq Joty
NTU
Singapore
srjoty@ntu.edu.sg

Giuseppe Carenini
UBC
Canada
carenini@cs.ubc.ca

Abstract

1 Tutorial Overview

The primary goal of this tutorial is for attendees to learn about recent work applying NLP to spoken and written conversations, with a focus on computational models for three related topics: conversational structure, summarization and sentiment detection, and group dynamics. We provide examples of specific NLP tasks within those three areas, how they relate to one another, their applications, and how we evaluate task performance.

We will begin by discussing motivations and applications of applying NLP methods to conversations, including downstream applications that could benefit. Attendees will hear about the challenges of working with noisy data, and examples of datasets of spoken and/or written conversations.

The first part of the tutorial covers **conversational structures**, the basic building blocks for working with conversational data. Participants will learn about computational methods for uncovering thread and topic structures of a conversation, detecting dialogue acts and adjacency pairs, identifying participant roles (where relevant), and how to treat disfluencies. We will cover methods for both synchronous (e.g., meeting, phone) and asynchronous (e.g., forum, email) conversations.

In the second part of the tutorial, we will focus on **sentiment analysis and summarization**. Attendees will learn about the related, overlapping tasks of detecting sentiment, subjectivity, and opinions. We will cover unsupervised and supervised approaches, as well as multimodal sentiment detection. Participants will learn about intrinsic vs. extrinsic evaluation of sentiment analysis methods for conversations.

For summarization, we will cover core topics, such as the notions of extractive vs. abstractive summarization, and summarization vs. compression. In particular, participants will learn about the limits of extractive summarization on noisy and opinion-filled conversation data. We will particularly emphasize the question of how to evaluate automatically generated summaries, including some of the controversial history surrounding automatic summarization metrics that are widely used.

In the final part of the tutorial, participants will learn about the growing field of research that uses NLP and machine learning methods to model and predict **group dynamics**, including prediction of group performance and participant affect. Attendees will learn about the close relationship between these three areas of summarization, sentiment, and group dynamics, and why researchers in each one of those areas often end up being concerned with the other two topics as well. Finally, we will discuss promising current and future directions of applying NLP to conversations.

2 Tutorial Outline

Introduction

- Types of conversational data (e.g., meetings, discussion forums, email)
- Challenges of conversational data
- Working with both spoken and written data

- Examples of conversational datasets (e.g., AMI, ELEA, BC3, Ubuntu Dialogs)
- Applications:
  - meeting support
  - social media analytics
  - business intelligence
  - people analytics / HR analytics
  - computational social science

Part 1: Building Blocks (Conversational Structures)

- Synchronous & asynchronous conversations
- Thread detection & conversation disentanglement
- Dialogue act & adjacency pairs
- Role detection
- Treating disfluencies

Part 2: Sentiment and Summarization

Sentiment

- Concepts and terminology: sentiment, subjectivity, polarity, and opinions
- Annotation schemes
- Annotated datasets (e.g., MPQA, AMI, BC3, Congressional floor debates, CMU-MOSI)
- Sentiment detection approaches:
  - lexicon-based
  - supervised approaches
  - unsupervised approaches
  - fine-grained vs. coarse-grained
  - multimodal sentiment detection
- Evaluation Metrics and Approaches (e.g., intrinsic vs. extrinsic)
- Applications
- Negative sentiment in face-to-face vs. online conversations

Summarization

- Concepts and terminology:
  - Abstraction vs. Extraction
  - Indicative vs. Informative
  - Summarization vs. Compression
- Summarization approaches:
  - Unsupervised extraction
  - Supervised extraction
  - NLG-based abstraction

  - Hybrid methods
  - Neural methods

- Evaluation Metrics and Approaches
  - ROUGE
  - Pyramids
  - Weighted precision-recall-fscore
  - Extrinsic evaluation
  - Human judgment, crowd-sourcing

- Annotated datasets (e.g., ICSI, AMI, BC3)

- The limits of extraction for conversational data

- The challenges of summarizing subjective data

Part 3: Group Dynamics

- Concepts and terminology: groups, dyads, task-centered groups

- Detecting emergent leadership from group discussion

- Measuring participant satisfaction

- Measuring group progress and performance

- Group cohesion

- Markov rewards analysis for group conversation data

- Social network analysis + NLP for small groups

- NLP and group conflict

- Datasets for analyzing speech/language and group interaction/performance (e.g. AMI, ELEA, Leadership corpus, Team Entrainment corpus)

3 Instructors

Dr. Gabriel Murray	Dr. Shafiq Joty	Dr. Giuseppe Carenini
Associate Professor	Assistant Professor	Associate Professor
Computer Information Systems	Computer Science & Eng.	Computer Science
University of the Fraser Valley	Nanyang Technological University	University of British Columbia
Abbotsford, Canada	Singapore	Vancouver, Canada
gabriel.murray@ufv.ca	srjoty@ntu.edu.sg	carenini@cs.ubc.ca

Dr. Gabriel Murray is an Associate Professor in Computer Information Systems at the University of the Fraser Valley (UFV), and an Affiliate Professor in CS at University of British Columbia (UBC). His background is in computational linguistics and multimodal speech and language processing. He holds a PhD in Informatics from the University of Edinburgh, completed under the supervision of Drs. Steve Renals and Johanna Moore. His research has focused on various aspects of multimodal conversational data, including automatic summarization and sentiment detection for group discussions. Recent research also focuses on predicting group performance and participant affect in conversational data. In 2011, Gabriel co-authored the book "Methods for Mining and Summarizing Text Conversations." He is the recipient of an NSERC Discovery grant on developing and applying machine learning methods for small group interaction.

Dr. Shafiq Joty is an Assistant Professor at the School of Computer Science and Engineering, NTU. Previously, he was a research scientist at the Qatar Computing Research Institute (QCRI). He holds a PhD in Computer Science from the University of British Columbia. His work has primarily focused on developing discourse analysis tools (e.g., discourse parser, coherence model, topic model, dialogue act recognizer), and exploiting these tools effectively in downstream NLP applications like machine translation, summarization, and sentiment analysis. Apart from discourse and its applications, he has also developed novel machine learning models for question answering, machine translation, and opinion analysis. Shafiq is a recipient of NSERC CGS-D scholarship and Microsoft Research Excellent Intern award.

Dr. Giuseppe Carenini is an Associate Professor in Computer Science at UBC. Giuseppe has broad interdisciplinary interests. His work on natural language processing and information visualization to support decision making has been published in over 100 peer-reviewed papers (including best paper at UMAP-14 and ACM-TiiS-14). Dr. Carenini was the area chair for "Sentiment Analysis, Opinion Mining, and Text Classification" of ACL 2009, the area chair for "Summarization and Generation" of NAACL 2012, the Program Co-Chair for IUI 2015, and the Program Co-Chair for SigDial 2016. He has also co-edited an ACM-TIST Special Issue on "Intelligent Visual Interfaces for Text Analysis." In 2011, he published a co-authored book on "Methods for Mining and Summarizing Text Conversations" (**?**). In his work, Dr. Carenini has also extensively collaborated with industrial partners, including Microsoft and IBM. Giuseppe was awarded a Google Research Award, an IBM CASCON Best Exhibit Award, and a Yahoo Faculty Research Award in 2007, 2010 and 2016 respectively.

Practical Parsing for Downstream Applications

Daniel Dakota & Sandra Kübler
Indiana University
{ddakota,skuebler}@indiana.edu

1 Overview

Parsing is a fundamental aspect for many NLP applications. However, it is often nor clear how to best incorporate parsers in downstream applications. Using parsers off the shelf is simple but often leads to bad performance. But even for researchers familiar with parsing and language issues, there are many decisions, often overlooked, concerning the algorithms themselves as well as the interaction between parser and language/treebank. This tutorial is intended to give researchers not familiar with parsing a better understanding of the practical implications of the individual decisions made when using parsers for their downstream application. We will cover dependency as well as constituent parsers.

In the tutorial, we will cover topics that walk a potential parsing user through the different steps from choosing between dependencies and constituents, choosing a parser, preprocessing, parser parameters, postprocessing, to evaluation and domain adaptation. We want to make sure that dialogs like the following do not happen as often anymore:

> "I am working on question answering for medical texts, and one of the problems we encounter is that the answer is often present, but in a different form from what we expected."
>
> "Sounds like a syntax problem. Have you tried using a parser?"
>
> "Yup, we took the XX parser with the pretrained model for English, but the results were really bad, so we gave up on that idea."
>
> "Have you tried retraining the parser for the medical domain?"
>
> "No, why? It comes with a pretrained model ..."

1.1 Parsing Issues

There are two components to parsing, the theoretical components, such as understanding PCFG, dependency grammars, and individual algorithms used in various parsers, and the practical and applied components, such as treebanks, POS tags, and evaluation. In order to choose the best parser for a given application, we need to understand both parts. Especially the practical component is often overlooked.

For many downstream applications, parsing is performed in order to perform various types of information extraction. However, as any degradation in performance at one step is compounded by any degradation in the next step, it is important to maximize performance, particularly early in a pipeline. Using an off the self parser is practical and efficient, but we need to understand which decisions are made implicitly in this choice, and that there are other options. Researchers need to understand how to create a new grammar, including the multitude of decisions involved in this step. Unfortunately, many of the quirks and oddities between parsers and data sets are not well known outside the parsing community, many of which have a rather substantial impact on performance.

This tutorial targets researchers who are interested in using parsers rather than investigating parsing issues. We will provide practical guidelines to better utilize existing parser for other research purposes. This includes covering different types of parsers and parsing resources. We will briefly review the theory behind types of parsing before moving on to three points of emphasis: what to know before prior to training, what to know about training, and what to know after during the testing/usage phase.

Before training a new grammar, a solid understanding of the domain and preprocessing standards of individual treebanks as well as an understanding as to what the parser needs to extract. The last point in particular is of great importance for choosing the most appropriate parser. A better understanding of treebank particulars is important. For many treebanks, particular preprocessing decisions need to be performed, which have a drastic impact on performance. We will examine various decisions, ranging from MWEs to removing null nodes or crossing branches/dependencies.

Training a grammar is the next step. Fine-tuning parameters is important for reaching good performance, but it involves much trial and error. And it requires a basic understanding of the the parameters and how they impact training. Furthermore, there may be unintended consequences or surprising results because of an interaction of parameters. Additionally, there are such considerations as the POS tags, function labels, and the domain relevant issues of the text.

After having trained a grammar, various postprocessing decisions need to be considered. This is particularly important for experiments that involve comparing against a gold standard, such as the original treebank. Understanding various evaluation metrics and procedures and how these can alter results is particularly important in order to ensure replicability and comparability.

The final goal of the tutorial is to provide a better understanding of how to best use parsers efficiently for downstream applications, including the basics for make better, more informed decisions. This will in turn produce better research, as improved parsing results depend on more attention to how very small details and decisions at the parsing stage can produce very different results and on the understanding that settings are not transferable across domains or languages. The tutorial will provide a starting point to making informed decisions in the most important aspects of parsing.

2 Outline

- Introduction
  - Outline of Tutorial
  - Purpose
  - Goal
- Which parser should I use?
  - Dependency Parsing
  - Constituency Parsing
- What do I have to do before training?
  - Treebanks/Data
  - Domains
  - Preprocessing
    - MWEs
    - Crossing Branches
    - Null Nodes
  - Goal of parser (e.g. syntactic or semantic information)
- What do I need to consider in training?
  - Algorithms
  - Parameters
  - Grammatical Functions
  - Training Sizes
  - POS Tags

- What should I do after parsing?
  - Postprocessing
  - Evaluation
- What is being parsed?
- How do I use all those parsers?
  - Dependency Parser (MATE Tools, TurboParser)
  - Constituency Parser (Berkeley, Lorg, Stanford)
  - NN Parser
  - Domain Specific parsers (Twitter parser)

3 Instructors

Daniel Dakota (ddakota@indiana.edu, cl.indiana.edu/~ddakota) is a sixth year doctoral student at Indiana University, USA and currently works as an AI Expert at Centogene in Berlin, Germany. His area of specialization is parsing morphologically rich languages with a particular focus on German. His thesis focuses on using distributional word representations to reduce data sparsity for the constituency parsing of German. He has secondary research interests in sentiment analysis and semantic processing and more recent interests in biomedical text processing.

Sandra Kübler (skuebler@indiana.edu, cl.indiana.edu/~skuebler) is a professor of Computational Linguistics at Indiana University, USA. Her research interests include parsing for morphologically rich languages, with a focus on German and Semitic languages. She was involved in the organization of the two SPMRL shared tasks on parsing morphologically rich languages, and was a guest co-editor of the special issue on that topic in Computational Linguistics.

Frame Semantics across Languages: Towards a Multilingual FrameNet

Collin F. Baker[1] **Michael Ellsworth**[1] **Miriam R. L. Petruck**[1] **Swabha Swayamdipta**[2]

1. International Computer Science Institute, 1947 Center St. Suite 600, Berkeley, California, 94704
2. Carnegie Mellon University, 5000 Forbes Ave, Pittsburgh, PA, 15213
{collinb,infinity,miriamp}@icsi.berkeley.edu, swabha@cs.cmu.edu

Abstract

FrameNet is a lexical resource that provides rich semantic representations of the core English vocabulary based on Fillmore's Frame Semantics, with more than 200k manually annotated examples. Resources based on FrameNet have now been created for roughly a dozen languages. This workshop will present current research on aligning Frame Semantic resources across languages and automatic frame semantic parsing in English and other languages. We will explore the extent to which semantic frames are similar across languages and the implications for theories of semantic universals, the practice of translation (whether human or machine), and multilingual knowledge representation. Does not require prior familiarity with Frame Semantics.

1 Description

The FrameNet Project at the International Computer Science Institute (ICSI, http://framenet.icsi.berkeley.edu) has created a detailed lexical database of contemporary English, (currently more than 13,000 lexical units in 1,200 semantic frames) based on Frame Semantics (Fillmore (1977), (1985)). NLP researchers have shown that such representations are useful in diverse applications such as question answering, text-to-scene systems, dialog systems, and social network extraction. Separate research projects have now developed Frame Semantic lexical databases for roughly a dozen languages (including Brazilian Portuguese, Chinese, Hebrew, Japanese, Korean, and Swedish) based in varying degrees on the original FrameNet structure, methodology and annotation practices (Ruppenhofer et al., 2016). Most have taken the ICSI English frames as a starting point and have found that the majority of target-language words fit comfortably in those frames.

The FrameNet team is developing alignments across these FrameNets, seeking to understand cross-linguistic similarities and differences in framing. Going beyond alignments between frames, we also use techniques such as multilingual word vectors (Hermann and Blunsom, 2014) to cluster and align lexical units (each a single sense of a word in a frame) across languages. The underlying research questions include: To what extent are semantic frames the same cross-culturally and cross-linguistically? Where they differ, what are the reasons for these differences? Will translations to be "frame preserving"?

This tutorial will discuss the methodology and status of the alignment effort, and of a recently launched parallel manual annotation task, and theoretical issues that have emerged in this area of research, including the interplay between semantic frames and constructions in different languages. We will also report on the state of the art in automatic frame semantic role labeling for English (Swayamdipta et al., 2017) and for other languages. This can be regarded as a structured prediction task which maps a sentence to a graph with nodes for each predicator and its arguments and adjuncts, linked by arcs representing the frame semantic roles. Recent approaches rely on neural architectures to learn representations which enforce global consistency for each classification decision and can learn from disparate data.

Participants in this tutorial will learn about:

1. Multilingual FrameNet, its methodology and practices

2. Cross-linguistic similarities and differences among the languages

3. Principles and challenges of multilingual lexical alignment
4. Issues of representation in frame vs. constructional analyses
5. Recent advances in Frame Semantic parsing (a.k.a. Frame Semantic role labeling)
6. Potential Applications of multilingual FrameNet databases

2 Outline of Tutorial

- Frame Semantics and FrameNet (Miriam R. L. Petruck)
  - Frames, Frame Elements (roles), and Lexical Units
  - Annotation and Reports
  - Frame Relations and Frame Element Relations
  - Construction Grammar and Constructicons
  - Constructions implicit in FrameNet Annotation
- The Multilingual FrameNet Project (Collin Baker)
  - FrameNets in Languages other than English
  - Variations in Sources, Goals, and Practices
  - Interactions between Frames and Constructions
  - Alignment across Languages
  - Alignment Algorithms and Results
- Cross-lingual Semantics (Michael Ellsworth)
  - Web Annotation Tool (Matos and Torrent, 2016)
  - Parallel Annotation on the TED Talk
  - Cross-lingual Framing Differences
  - Metaphor and Metonymy in FrameNet
  - Frame-based Knowledge Representation
  - Mental Spaces: Negation and Conditionals
- ASRL and Multilingual FrameNet Applications (Swabha Swayamdipta)
  - Automatic Frame Semantic Role Labeling (English)
  - Automatic Frame Semantic Role Labeling (Other Languages)
  - Potential Multilingual Applications

3 Instructors

Collin F. Baker

Collin F. Baker (International Computer Science Institute, collinb@icsi.berkeley.edu, `https://www.icsi.berkeley.edu/icsi/people/collinb`) has been affiliated with the FrameNet Project since it began, Project Manager, 2000-present), working closely with the late Charles J. Fillmore and many collaborators. He was also Project Manger of the MetaNet Project at ICSI (2012-2015, `http://metanet.icsi.berkeley.edu`), an IARPA-funded effort to recognize metaphoric language automatically in several languages. His research interests include building and aligning FrameNets across languages (Lönneker-Rodman and Baker (2009), Gilardi and Baker (2017)), aligning FrameNet to other lexical resources (Fellbaum and Baker (2013), (2008), Ferrández et al. (2010)) and linking to ontologies and reasoning (Scheffczyk et al., 2010).

Michael Ellsworth

Michael Ellsworth (Addeco/International Computer Science Institute, (infinity@icsi.berkeley.edu, `https://berkeley.academia.edu/MichaelEllsworth`) has been involved in lexical semantic research for nearly 20 years, and has been a key member of the FrameNet team, involved in frame definition, annotation, annotator training, and data-integrity checking; he has been in charge of the ontology-like hierarchy that organizes the frames since 2002. Publication topics include the differences between FrameNet and other annotation projects (Ellsworth et al., 2004), the FrameNet hierarchy and ontologies (Dolbey et al., 2006), the principles behind FrameNet annotation, paraphrasing using FrameNet (Ellsworth and Janin, 2007), and various English grammatical constructions (Lee-Goldman et al., 2009). He is currently writing a dissertation on how the domain of emotion is encoded in English words and grammatical constructions.

Miriam R. L. Petruck

Miriam R. L. Petruck (International Computer Science Institute, miriamp@icsi.berkeley.edu, `https://www.icsi.berkeley.edu/icsi/people/miriamp`) received her Ph.D. in Linguistics from the University of California, Berkeley, CA, under the direction of the late Charles J. Fillmore. A key member of the FrameNet development team almost since the project's founding in 1997, her research interests include semantics (Petruck (2009),(1996)), lexical semantics (Petruck and Ellsworth, 2016), knowledge base development, grammar and lexis, semantics, Frame Semantics and Construction Grammar, particularly as these linguistic theories support advances in NLU and NLP. She is a frequent invited speaker, lecturing internationally about Frame Semantics, Construction Grammar, and FrameNet. Petruck is currently working on a manuscript about FrameNet and NLP.

Swabha Swayamdipta

Swabha Swayamdipta (swabha@cs.cmu.edu, `http://www.cs.cmu.edu/~sswayamd`) is a PhD student at the Language Technologies Institute at Carnegie Mellon University (currently a visiting student at U Washington). She works with Noah Smith and Chris Dyer on developing efficient algorithms for broad-coverage semantic parsing, with a focus on exploiting the relationship between syntax and semantics (Swayamdipta et al., 2017). She has a Masters degree from Columbia University, and was a research intern at Google New York. Her research interests also include applications of broad-coverage semantics for tasks such as entailment and coreference.

References

Andrew Dolbey, Michael Ellsworth, and Jan Scheffczyk. 2006. BioFrameNet: A Domain-Specific FrameNet Extension with Links to Biomedical Ontologies. In *Proceedings of KR-MED*.

Michael Ellsworth and Adam Janin. 2007. Mutaphrase: Paraphrasing with FrameNet. In *Proceedings of the Workshop on Textual Entailment and Paraphrasing*, Prague, June. Association for Computational Linguistics.

Michael Ellsworth, Katrin Erk, Paul Kingsbury, and Sebastian Padó. 2004. PropBank, SALSA, and FrameNet: How Design Determines Product. In *Proceedings of the LREC 2004 Workshop on Building Lexical Resources from Semantically Annotated Corpora*, Lisbon, Portugal.

Christiane Fellbaum and Collin F. Baker. 2008. Can WordNet and FrameNet be Made "Interoperable"? In *Proceedings of The First International Conference on Global Interoperability for Language Resources*, pages 67–74.

Christiane Fellbaum and Collin Baker. 2013. Comparing and harmonizing different verb classifications in light of a semantic annotation task. *Linguistics*, 51(4):707–728.

Óscar Ferrández, Michael Ellsworth, Rafael Muñoz, and Collin F. Baker. 2010. Aligning FrameNet and WordNet based on Semantic Neighborhoods. In Nicoletta Calzolari (Conference Chair), Khalid Choukri, Bente Maegaard, Joseph Mariani, Jan Odjik, Stelios Piperidis, Mike Rosner, and Daniel Tapias, editors, *Proceedings of the Seventh conference on International Language Resources and Evaluation (LREC'10)*, pages 310–314, Valletta, Malta, may. European Language Resources Association (ELRA).

Charles J. Fillmore. 1977. The need for a frame semantics in linguistics. In Hans Karlgren, editor, *Statistical Methods in Linguistics*. Scriptor.

Charles J. Fillmore. 1985. Frames and the semantics of understanding. *Quaderni di Semantica*, 6(2):222–254.

Luca Gilardi and Collin F. Baker. 2017. Learning to align across languages: Toward multilingual framenet. In Tiago Timponi Torrent, Lars Borin, and Collin F. Baker, editors, *Proceedings of the International FrameNet Workshop 2018: Multilingual FrameNets and Constructicons*. LREC.

Karl Moritz Hermann and Phil Blunsom. 2014. Multilingual models for compositional distributed semantics. In *Proceedings of the 52nd Annual Meeting of the Association for Computational Linguistics (Volume 1: Long Papers)*, pages 58–68. Association for Computational Linguistics.

Russell Lee-Goldman, Russell Rhodes, and Michael Ellsworth. 2009. Determination and modification: interaction and interpretation. San Francisco, January. Linguistic Society of America. Presented at annual meeting.

Birte Lönneker-Rodman and Collin F. Baker. 2009. The FrameNet Model and its Applications. *Natural Language Engineering*, 15(03):415–453.

Ely Matos and Tiago Torrent. 2016. A flexible tool for an enriched FrameNet. In *9th International Conference on Construction Grammar (ICCG9)*. Federal University of Juiz de Fora.

Miriam R L Petruck and Michael Ellsworth. 2016. Representing support verbs in framenet. In *Proceedings of the 12th Workshop on Multiword Expressions*, pages 72–77. Association for Computational Linguistics.

Miriam R. L. Petruck. 1996. Frame Semantics. In Jef Verschueren, Jan-Ola Östman, Jan Blommaert, and Chris Bulcaen, editors, *Handbook of Pragmatics*. John Benjamins.

Miriam Petruck. 2009. Typological Considerations in constructing a Hebrew FrameNet. In Hans C. Boas, editor, *Multilingual FrameNets in Computational Lexicography*, pages 183–205. Mouton.

Josef Ruppenhofer, Michael Ellsworth, Miriam R. L. Petruck, Christopher R. Johnson, Collin F. Baker, and Jan Scheffczyk. 2016. *FrameNet II: Extended Theory and Practice*. International Computer Science Institute, Berkeley, California. Revised Nov. 1, 2016. Distributed with the FrameNet data.

Jan Scheffczyk, Collin F. Baker, and Srini Narayanan. 2010. Reasoning over Natural Language Text by Means of FrameNet and Ontologies. In Chu-Ren Huang, Nicoletta Calzolari, Aldo Gangemi, Alessandro Lenci, Alessandro Oltramari, and Laurent Prévot, editors, *Ontology and the Lexicon: A Natural Language Processing Perspective*, Studies in Natural Language Processing, chapter 4, pages 53–71. Cambridge University Press, Cambridge, UK. Expanded version of paper at OntoLex, 2006. (ISBN-13: 9780521886598).

Swabha Swayamdipta, Sam Thomson, Chris Dyer, and Noah A. Smith. 2017. Frame-semantic parsing with softmax-margin segmental rnns and a syntactic scaffold.

Deep Bayesian Learning and Understanding

Jen-Tzung Chien
Department of Electrical and Computer Engineering
National Chiao Tung University, Hsinchu, Taiwan
jtchien@nctu.edu.tw

1 Motivation

Given the current growth in research and related emerging technologies in machine learning and deep learning, it is timely to introduce this tutorial to a large number of researchers and practitioners who are attending COLING 2018 and working on statistical models, deep neural networks, sequential learning and natural language understanding. To the best of our knowledge, there is no similar tutorial presented in previous ACL/COLING/EMNLP/NAACL. This three-hour tutorial will concentrate on a wide range of theories and applications and systematically present the recent advances in deep Bayesian and sequential learning which are impacting the communities of computational linguistics, human language technology and machine learning for natural language processing.

2 Tutorial description

This tutorial introduces the advances in deep Bayesian learning with abundant applications for natural language understanding ranging from speech recognition (Saon and Chien, 2012; Chan et al., 2016) to document summarization (Chang and Chien, 2009), text classification (Blei et al., 2003; Zhang et al., 2015), text segmentation (Chien and Chueh, 2012), information extraction (Narasimhan et al., 2016), image caption generation (Vinyals et al., 2015; Xu et al., 2015), sentence generation (Li et al., 2016b), dialogue control (Zhao and Eskenazi, 2016; Li et al., 2016a), sentiment classification, recommendation system, question answering (Sukhbaatar et al., 2015) and machine translation (Bahdanau et al., 2014), to name a few. Traditionally, "deep learning" is taken to be a learning process where the inference or optimization is based on the real-valued deterministic model. The "semantic structure" in words, sentences, entities, actions and documents drawn from a large vocabulary may not be well expressed or correctly optimized in mathematical logic or computer programs. The "distribution function" in discrete or continuous latent variable model for natural language may not be properly decomposed or estimated in model inference. This tutorial addresses the fundamentals of statistical models and neural networks, and focus on a series of advanced Bayesian models and deep models including hierarchical Dirichlet process (Teh et al., 2006), Chinese restaurant process (Blei et al., 2010), hierarchical Pitman-Yor process (Teh, 2006), Indian buffet process (Ghahramani and Griffiths, 2005), recurrent neural network (Mikolov et al., 2010; Van Den Oord et al., 2016), long short-term memory (Hochreiter and Schmidhuber, 1997; Cho et al., 2014), sequence-to-sequence model (Sutskever et al., 2014), variational auto-encoder (Kingma and Welling, 2014), generative adversarial network (Goodfellow et al., 2014), attention mechanism (Chorowski et al., 2015; Seo et al., 2016), memory-augmented neural network (Graves et al., 2014; Graves et al., 2014), stochastic neural network (Bengio et al., 2014; Miao et al., 2016), predictive state neural network (Downey et al., 2017), policy gradient (Yu et al., 2017) and reinforcement learning (Mnih et al., 2015). We present how these models are connected and why they work for a variety of applications on symbolic and complex patterns in natural language. The variational inference and sampling method are formulated to tackle the optimization for complicated models (Rezende et al., 2014). The word and sentence embeddings, clustering and co-clustering are merged with linguistic and semantic constraints. A series of case studies are presented to tackle different issues in deep Bayesian learning and understanding. At last, we point out a number of directions and outlooks for future studies.

3 Tutorial outline

- Introduction
  - Motivation and background
  - Probabilistic models
  - Neural networks
  - Modern natural language models
- Bayesian Learning
  - Inference and optimization
  - Variational Bayesian (VB) inference
  - Monte Carlo Markov chain (MCMC) inference
  - Bayesian nonparametrics (BNP)
  - Hierarchical theme and topic model
  - Hierarchical Pitman-Yor-Dirichlet process
  - Nested Indian buffet process
- Deep Learning
  - Deep unfolded topic model
  - Gated recurrent neural network
  - Bayesian recurrent neural network (RNN) (Coffee Break)
  - Sequence-to-sequence learning
  - Convolutional neural network (CNN)
  - Dilated recurrent neural network
  - Generative adversarial network (GAN)
  - Variational auto-encoder (VAE)
- Advances in Deep Sequential Learning
  - Memory-augmented neural network
  - Neural variational text processing
  - Neural discrete representation learning
  - Recurrent ladder network
  - Stochastic recurrent network
  - Predictive-state recurrent neural network
  - Sequence generative adversarial network
  - Deep reinforcement learning & understanding
- Summarization and Future Trend

4 Description of tutorial content

The presentation of this tutorial is arranged into five parts. First of all, we share the current status of researches on natural language understanding, statistical modeling and deep neural network and explain the key issues in deep Bayesian learning for discrete-valued observation data and latent semantics. A new paradigm called the symbolic neural learning is introduced to extend how data analysis is performed from language processing to semantic learning and memory networking. Secondly, we address a number of Bayesian models ranging from latent variable model to VB inference (Chien and Chang, 2014; Chien and Chueh, 2011; Chien, 2015b), MCMC sampling (Watanabe and Chien, 2015) and BNP learning (Chien,

2016; Chien, 2015a; Chien, 2018) for hierarchical, thematic and sparse topics from natural language. In the third part, a series of deep models including deep unfolding (Chien and Lee, 2018), Bayesian RNN (Gal and Ghahramani, 2016; Chien and Ku, 2016), sequence-to-sequence learning (Graves et al., 2006; Gehring et al., 2017), CNN (Kalchbrenner et al., 2014; Xingjian et al., 2015; Dauphin et al., 2017), GAN (Tsai and Chien, 2017) and VAE are introduced. The coffee break is arranged within this part. Next, the fourth part focuses on a variety of advanced studies which illustrate how deep Bayesian learning is developed to infer the sophisticated recurrent models for natural language understanding. In particular, the memory network (Weston et al., 2015; Chien and Lin, 2018), neural variational learning (Serban et al., 2017; Chung et al., 2015), neural discrete representation (Jang et al., 2016; Maddison et al., 2016; van den Oord et al., 2017), recurrent ladder network (Rasmus et al., 2015; Prémont-Schwarz et al., 2017; Sønderby et al., 2016), stochastic neural network (Fraccaro et al., 2016; Goyal et al., 2017; Shabanian et al., 2017), Markov recurrent neural network (Venkatraman et al., 2017; Kuo and Chien, 2018), sequence GAN (Yu et al., 2017) and reinforcement learning (Tegho et al., 2017) are introduced in various deep models which open a window to more practical tasks, e.g. reading comprehension, sentence generation, dialogue system, question answering and machine translation. In the final part, we spotlight on some future directions for deep language understanding which can handle the challenges of big data, heterogeneous condition and dynamic system. In particular, deep learning, structural learning, temporal modeling, long history representation and stochastic learning are emphasized. Slides of this tutorial are available at http://chien.cm.nctu.edu.tw/home/coling/.

5 Instructor

Jen-Tzung Chien received his Ph.D. degree in electrical engineering from National Tsing Hua University, Hsinchu, Taiwan, in 1997. He is now with the Department of Electrical and Computer Engineering and the Department of Computer Science at the National Chiao Tung University, Hsinchu, where he is currently a Chair Professor. He was a visiting researcher with the IBM T. J. Watson Research Center, Yorktown Heights, NY, in 2010. His research interests include machine learning, deep learning, natural language processing and computer vision. Dr. Chien served as the associate editor of the IEEE Signal Processing Letters in 2008-2011, the guest editor of the IEEE Transactions on Audio, Speech and Language Processing in 2012, the organization committee member of ICASSP 2009, ISCSLP 2016, the area coordinator of Interspeech 2012, EUSIPCO 2017, 2018, the program chair of ISCSLP 2018, the general chair of MLSP 2017, and currently serves as an elected member of IEEE Machine Learning for Signal Processing Technical Committee. He received the Best Paper Award of IEEE Automatic Speech Recognition and Understanding Workshop in 2011 and the AAPM Farrington Daniels Paper Award in 2018. He has published extensively including the book "Bayesian Speech and Language Processing", Cambridge University Press, 2015. He was the tutorial speaker for APSIPA 2013, ISCSLP 2014, Interspeech 2013, 2016 and ICASSP 2012, 2015 and 2017. (http://chien.cm.nctu.edu.tw/)

References

Dzmitry Bahdanau, Kyunghyun Cho, and Yoshua Bengio. 2014. Neural machine translation by jointly learning to align and translate. *arXiv preprint arXiv:1409.0473*.

Yoshua Bengio, Eric Thibodeau-Laufer, Guillaume Alain, and Jason Yosinski. 2014. Deep generative stochastic networks trainable by backprop. In *Proc. of International Conference on Machine Learning*.

David M. Blei, Andrew Y. Ng, and Michael I. Jordan. 2003. Latent Dirichlet allocation. *Journal of Machine Learning Research*, 3(3):993–1022, Jan.

David M. Blei, Thomas L. Griffiths, and Michael I. Jordan. 2010. The nested Chinese restaurant process and Bayesian nonparametric inference of topic hierarchies. *Journal of the ACM*, 57(2). Article 7.

W. Chan, N. Jaitly, Q. Le, and O. Vinyals. 2016. Listen, attend and spell: A neural network for large vocabulary conversational speech recognition. In *Proc. of IEEE International Conference on Acoustics, Speech and Signal Processing*, pages 4960–4964.

Ying-Lang Chang and Jen-Tzung Chien. 2009. Latent Dirichlet learning for document summarization. In *Proc. of IEEE International Conference on Acoustics, Speech and Signal Processing*, pages 1689–1692.

Jen-Tzung Chien and Ying-Lan Chang. 2014. Bayesian sparse topic model. *Journal of Signal Processing Systems*, 74(3):375–389.

Jen-Tzung Chien and Chuang-Hua Chueh. 2011. Dirichlet class language models for speech recognition. *IEEE Transactions on Audio, Speech, and Language Processing*, 19(3):482–495.

Jen-Tzung Chien and Chuang-Hua Chueh. 2012. Topic-based hierarchical segmentation. *IEEE Transactions on Audio, Speech, and Language Processing*, 20(1):55–66.

Jen-Tzung Chien and Yuan-Chu Ku. 2016. Bayesian recurrent neural network for language modeling. *IEEE Transactions on Neural Networks and Learning Systems*, 27(2):361–374.

Jen-Tzung Chien and Chao-Hsi Lee. 2018. Deep unfolding for topic models. *IEEE Transactions on Pattern Analysis and Machine Intelligence*, 40(2):318–331.

Jen-Tzung Chien and Ting-An Lin. 2018. Supportive attention in end-to-end memory networks. In *Proc. of IEEE International Workshop on Machine Learning for Signal Processing*, pages 1–6.

Jen-Tzung Chien. 2015a. Hierarchical Pitman-Yor-Dirichlet language model. *IEEE/ACM Transactions on Audio, Speech, and Language Processing*, 23(8):1259–1272.

Jen-Tzung Chien. 2015b. Laplace group sensing for acoustic models. *IEEE/ACM Transactions on Audio, Speech, and Language Processing*, 23(5):909–922.

Jen-Tzung Chien. 2016. Hierarchical theme and topic modeling. *IEEE Transactions on Neural Networks and Learning Systems*, 27(3):565–578.

Jen-Tzung Chien. 2018. Bayesian nonparametric learning for hierarchical and sparse topics. *IEEE/ACM Transactions on Audio, Speech, and Language Processing*, 26(2):422–435.

Kyunghyun Cho, Bart Van Merriënboer, Caglar Gulcehre, Dzmitry Bahdanau, Fethi Bougares, Holger Schwenk, and Yoshua Bengio. 2014. Learning phrase representations using RNN encoder-decoder for statistical machine translation. In *Proc. of Conference on Empirical Methods in Natural Language Processing*, pages 1724–1734.

Jan K Chorowski, Dzmitry Bahdanau, Dmitriy Serdyuk, Kyunghyun Cho, and Yoshua Bengio. 2015. Attention-based models for speech recognition. In *Advances in Neural Information Processing Systems*, pages 577–585.

Junyoung Chung, Kyle Kastner, Laurent Dinh, Kratarth Goel, Aaron C Courville, and Yoshua Bengio. 2015. A recurrent latent variable model for sequential data. In *Advances in Neural Information Processing Systems*, pages 2980–2988.

Yann N Dauphin, Angela Fan, Michael Auli, and David Grangier. 2017. Language modeling with gated convolutional networks. In *Proc. of International Conference on Machine Learning*, pages 933–941.

Carlton Downey, Ahmed Hefny, Byron Boots, Geoffrey J Gordon, and Boyue Li. 2017. Predictive state recurrent neural networks. In *Advances in Neural Information Processing Systems*, pages 6055–6066.

Marco Fraccaro, Søren Kaae Sø nderby, Ulrich Paquet, and Ole Winther. 2016. Sequential neural models with stochastic layers. In *Advances in Neural Information Processing Systems*, pages 2199–2207.

Yarin Gal and Zoubin Ghahramani. 2016. A theoretically grounded application of dropout in recurrent neural networks. In *Advances in Neural Information Processing Systems*, pages 1019–1027.

Jonas Gehring, Michael Auli, David Grangier, Denis Yarats, and Yann N Dauphin. 2017. Convolutional sequence to sequence learning. In *Proc. of International Conference on Machine Learning*, pages 1243–1252.

Zoubin Ghahramani and Thomas L. Griffiths. 2005. Infinite latent feature models and the Indian buffet process. In *Advances in Neural Information Processing Systems*, volume 18, pages 475–482.

Ian Goodfellow, Jean Pouget-Abadie, Mehdi Mirza, Bing Xu, David Warde-Farley, Sherjil Ozair, Aaron Courville, and Yoshua Bengio. 2014. Generative adversarial nets. In *Advances in Neural Information Processing Systems*, pages 2672–2680.

Anirudh Goyal, Alessandro Sordoni, Marc-Alexandre Côté, Nan Ke, and Yoshua Bengio. 2017. Z-forcing: Training stochastic recurrent networks. In *Advances in Neural Information Processing Systems 30*, pages 6713–6723.

Alex Graves, Santiago Fernández, Faustino Gomez, and Jürgen Schmidhuber. 2006. Connectionist temporal classification: labelling unsegmented sequence data with recurrent neural networks. In *Proc. of International Conference on Machine Learning*, pages 369–376.

Alex Graves, Greg Wayne, and Ivo Danihelka. 2014. Neural Turing machines. *arXiv preprint arXiv:1410.5401.*

Sepp Hochreiter and Jürgen Schmidhuber. 1997. Long short-term memory. *Neural Computation*, 9(8):1735–1780.

Eric Jang, Shixiang Gu, and Ben Poole. 2016. Categorical reparameterization with Gumbel-softmax. *arXiv preprint arXiv:1611.01144.*

Nal Kalchbrenner, Edward Grefenstette, and Phil Blunsom. 2014. A convolutional neural network for modelling sentences. In *Proc. of Annual Meeting of the Association for Computational Linguistics*, pages 655–665.

Diederik P Kingma and Max Welling. 2014. Auto-encoding variational Bayes. *arXiv preprint arXiv:1312.6114.*

Che-Yu Kuo and Jen-Tzung Chien. 2018. Markov recurrent neural networks. In *Proc. of IEEE International Workshop on Machine Learning for Signal Processing*, pages 1–6.

Jiwei Li, Alexander H Miller, Sumit Chopra, Marc'Aurelio Ranzato, and Jason Weston. 2016a. Learning through dialogue interactions by asking questions. *arXiv preprint arXiv:1612.04936.*

Jiwei Li, Will Monroe, Alan Ritter, and Dan Jurafsky. 2016b. Deep reinforcement learning for dialogue generation. In *Proc. of Conference on Empirical Methods in Natural Language Processing*, pages 1192–1202.

Chris J Maddison, Andriy Mnih, and Yee Whye Teh. 2016. The concrete distribution: A continuous relaxation of discrete random variables. *arXiv preprint arXiv:1611.00712.*

Yishu Miao, Lei Yu, and Phil Blunsom. 2016. Neural variational inference for text processing. In *Proc. of International Conference on Machine Learning*, pages 1727–1736.

Tomáš Mikolov, Martin Karafiát, Lukáš Burget, Jan Černocký, and Sanjeev Khudanpur. 2010. Recurrent neural network based language model. In *Proc. of Annual Conference of International Speech Communication Association*, pages 1045–1048, Sep.

Volodymyr Mnih, Koray Kavukcuoglu, David Silver, Andrei A Rusu, Joel Veness, Marc G Bellemare, Alex Graves, Martin Riedmiller, Andreas K Fidjeland, Georg Ostrovski, et al. 2015. Human-level control through deep reinforcement learning. *Nature*, 518(7540):529–533.

Karthik Narasimhan, Adam Yala, and Regina Barzilay. 2016. Improving information extraction by acquiring external evidence with reinforcement learning. In *Proc. of Conference on Empirical Methods in Natural Language Processing*, pages 2355–2365.

Isabeau Prémont-Schwarz, Alexander Ilin, Tele Hao, Antti Rasmus, Rinu Boney, and Harri Valpola. 2017. Recurrent ladder networks. In *Advances in Neural Information Processing Systems*, pages 6011–6021.

Antti Rasmus, Mathias Berglund, Mikko Honkala, Harri Valpola, and Tapani Raiko. 2015. Semi-supervised learning with ladder networks. In *Advances in Neural Information Processing Systems*, pages 3546–3554.

Danilo Jimenez Rezende, Shakir Mohamed, and Daan Wierstra. 2014. Stochastic backpropagation and approximate inference in deep generative models. In *Proc. of International Conference on Machine Learning*, pages 1278–1286.

George Saon and Jen-Tzung Chien. 2012. Large-vocabulary continuous speech recognition systems: A look at some recent advances. *IEEE Signal Processing Magazine*, 29(6):18–33, Nov.

Minjoon Seo, Aniruddha Kembhavi, Ali Farhadi, and Hannaneh Hajishirzi. 2016. Bidirectional attention flow for machine comprehension. *arXiv preprint arXiv:1611.01603.*

Iulian V. Serban, Alessandro Sordoni, Ryan Lowe, Laurent Charlin, Joelle Pineau, Aaron Courville, and Yoshua Bengio. 2017. A hierarchical latent variable encoder-decoder model for generating dialogues. In *Proc. of AAAI Conference on Artificial Intelligence*, pages 3295–3301.

Samira Shabanian, Devansh Arpit, Adam Trischler, and Yoshua Bengio. 2017. Variational Bi-LSTMs. *arXiv preprint arXiv:1711.05717.*

Casper Kaae Sønderby, Tapani Raiko, Lars Maaløe, Søren Kaae Sønderby, and Ole Winther. 2016. Ladder variational autoencoders. In *Advances in Neural Information Processing Systems*, pages 3738–3746.

Sainbayar Sukhbaatar, Arthur Szlam, Jason Weston, and Rob Fergus. 2015. End-to-end memory networks. In *Advances in Neural Information Processing Systems*, pages 2440–2448.

Ilya Sutskever, Oriol Vinyals, and Quoc V Le. 2014. Sequence to sequence learning with neural networks. In *Advances in Neural Information Processing Systems*, pages 3104–3112. .

Christopher Tegho, Paweł Budzianowski, and Milica Gašić. 2017. Uncertainty estimates for efficient neural network-based dialogue policy optimisation. *arXiv preprint arXiv:1711.11486.*

Yee Whye Teh, Michael I. Jordan, Matthew J. Beal, and David M. Blei. 2006. Hierarchical Dirichlet process. *Journal of the American Statistical Association*, 101(476):1566–1581, Dec.

Yee Whye Teh. 2006. A hierarchical Bayesian language model based on Pitman-Yor processes. In *Proc. of International Conference on Computational Linguistics and Annual Meeting of the Association for Computational Linguistics*, pages 985–992.

Jen-Chieh Tsai and Jen-Tzung Chien. 2017. Adversarial domain separation and adaptation. In *Proc. of IEEE International Workshop on Machine Learning for Signal Processing*, pages 1–6.

Aaron Van Den Oord, Sander Dieleman, Heiga Zen, Karen Simonyan, Oriol Vinyals, Alex Graves, Nal Kalchbrenner, Andrew Senior, and Koray Kavukcuoglu. 2016. Wavenet: A generative model for raw audio. *arXiv preprint arXiv:1609.03499.*

Aaron van den Oord, Oriol Vinyals, and Koray Kavukcuoglu. 2017. Neural discrete representation learning. In *Advances in Neural Information Processing Systems*, pages 6309–6318.

Arun Venkatraman, Nicholas Rhinehart, Wen Sun, Lerrel Pinto, Martial Hebert, Byron Boots, Kris Kitani, and J Bagnell. 2017. Predictive-state decoders: Encoding the future into recurrent networks. In *Advances in Neural Information Processing Systems*, pages 1172–1183.

Oriol Vinyals, Alexander Toshev, Samy Bengio, and Dumitru Erhan. 2015. Show and tell: A neural image caption generator. In *Proc. of IEEE Conference on Computer Vision and Pattern Recognition*, pages 3156–3164.

Shinji Watanabe and Jen-Tzung Chien. 2015. *Bayesian Speech and Language Processing*. Cambridge University Press.

Jason Weston, Sumit Chopra, and Antoine Bordes. 2015. Memory networks. In *Proc. of International Conference on Learning Representation.*

Shi Xingjian, Zhourong Chen, Hao Wang, Dit-Yan Yeung, Wai-kin Wong, and Wang-chun Woo. 2015. Convolutional LSTM network: A machine learning approach for precipitation nowcasting. In *Advances in Neural Information Processing Systems*, pages 802–810.

Kelvin Xu, Jimmy Ba, Ryan Kiros, Kyunghyun Cho, Aaron Courville, Ruslan Salakhudinov, Rich Zemel, and Yoshua Bengio. 2015. Show, attend and tell: Neural image caption generation with visual attention. In *Proc. of International Conference on Machine Learning*, pages 2048–2057.

Lantao Yu, Weinan Zhang, Jun Wang, and Yong Yu. 2017. SeqGAN: sequence generative adversarial nets with policy gradient. In *Prof. of AAAI Conference on Artificial Intelligence*, volume 31, pages 2852–2858.

Xiang Zhang, Junbo Zhao, and Yann LeCun. 2015. Character-level convolutional networks for text classification. In *Advances in Neural Information Processing Systems*, pages 649–657.

Tiancheng Zhao and Maxine Eskenazi. 2016. Towards end-to-end learning for dialog state tracking and management using deep reinforcement learning. *arXiv preprint arXiv:1606.02560.*

Data-Driven Text Simplification

Sanja Štajner
Data and Web Science Group
University of Mannheim, Germany
sanja@informatik.uni-mannheim.de

Horacio Saggion
TALN Research Group
Universitat Pompeu Fabra, Spain
horacio.saggion@upf.edu

Abstract

Automatic text simplification is the process of transforming a complex text into an equivalent version which would be easier to read or understand by a target audience, or easier to handle by automatic natural language processors. The transformation of the text would entail modifications at the vocabulary, syntax, and discourse levels of the text. Over the last years research in automatic text simplification has intensified not only in the number of human languages being addressed but also in the number of techniques being proposed to deal with it from initial rule-based approaches to current data-driven techniques. The aim of this tutorial is to provide a comprehensive overview of past and current research on automatic text simplification.

1 Introduction

Automatic text simplification (ATS) appeared as an area of research in natural language processing (NLP) in the late nineties (Chandrasekar et al., 1996). Its goal is to automatically transform given input (text or sentences) into a simpler variant without significantly changing the input original meaning (Saggion, 2017). What is considered a simpler variant clearly depends on who/what is the target readership/application. Initially, ATS was proposed as a pre-processing step to improve various NLP tasks, e.g. machine translation, information extraction, summarisation, and semantic role labeling. In such scenario, a simpler variant is the one that improves the performance of the targeted NLP task, when used instead of the original input text. Later, the main purpose of ATS systems shifted towards better social inclusion of people with various reading and cognitive impairments, e.g. people with low literacy levels, non-native speakers, people with aphasia, dyslexia, autism, or Down's syndrome. In that case, a simpler variant of a given text snippet would be the one that can be read faster and understood better by the target population.

Traditionally, two different tasks are considered in ATS (Saggion, 2018): lexical simplification is concerned with the modification of the complex or uncommon vocabulary of the text by replacing it with synonyms which are simpler to read or understand, while syntactic simplification is concerned with transforming sentences containing syntactic phenomena which may hinder readability and comprehension (e.g. complex subordination phenomena, passive voice constructions) into simpler equivalents.

Several ATS projects were conducted aimed at producing simplification systems for different audiences and languages. The PSET (Practical Simplification of English Texts) project was a UK initiative to produce adapted texts for aphasic people (Carroll et al., 1998). The PorSimples project (Aluisio et al., 2010) developed an automatic system and editing assistance tool to simplify texts for people with low literacy levels in Brazil. The Simplext project (Saggion et al., 2015) developed simplification technology for Spanish speakers with intellectual disabilities. The FIRST project (Martín-Valdivia et al., 2014) developed a semi-automatic text adaptation tool for English, Spanish and Bulgarian to improve accessibility of written texts to people with autism, while the Able to Include project (Saggion et al., 2017; Ferrés et al., 2016) targeted people with intellectual disabilities on the Web. All those projects had a strong multidisciplinary as well as social character, extending the limits of psycholinguistics, readability assessment, computational linguistics, and natural language processing. We will present the techniques used to transform written texts in each of those projects and make an in-depth discussion of what those projects had in common in terms of techniques and resources, and in what they differed.

1.1 Data-driven Paradigm in Simplification

With the emergence of Simple English Wikipedia and its (comparable) alignment with English Wikipedia, which for the first time offered a large parallel dataset for training of the ATS systems, the approaches to ATS shifted from rule-based (Siddharthan, 2006) to purely data-driven (Coster and Kauchak, 2011; Zhu et al., 2010; Kauchak, 2013), and later hybrid ones (Siddharthan and Mandya, 2014). It created opportunity for stronger NLP component of the systems and new challenges in text/sentence generation, but at the cost of blurring the final goal of those ATS systems, as there was no clear target population in mind anymore. The release of Newsela dataset (Xu et al., 2015) for English and Spanish in 2015, created opportunities for better modelling of simplification operations, given its well-controlled quality of manual simplifications at five different text complexity levels. Following the previously proposed idea of approaching ATS as a monolingual machine translation (MT) task (Specia, 2010; Coster and Kauchak, 2011), Xu et al. (2016) proposed an MT-based ATS system for English built upon Newsela and the large paraphrase database (Pavlick and Callison-Burch, 2016). The manual sentence alignment of English Newsela (Xu et al., 2015), improved automatic alignment of EW-SEW corpus (Hwang et al., 2015), and the recently released free tools for sentence alignment (Paetzold et al., 2017; Štajner et al., 2017; Štajner et al., 2018), offered new opportunities for data-driven ATS.

In 2017, several ATS systems exploring various deep learning architectures appeared, using the new alignments of Wikipedia and Newsela for training. Sequence-to-sequence neural models (Nisioi et al., 2017; Štajner and Nisioi, 2018), and the neural model based on reinforcement learning techniques (Zhang and Lapata, 2017) showed a dominance of neural ATS approaches over the previous data-driven approaches in terms of quality of generated output (better grammaticality and meaning preservation). The question of simplicity of the generated output and the adaptability of those models to different text genres and languages other than English, is still present. While solving the problems of grammaticality and meaning preservation, the neural TS systems introduced a new challenge, showing problems in dealing with abundance of name entities present both in news articles and Wikipedia articles.

2 Tutorial Overview

In this tutorial, we aim to provide an extensive overview of automatic text simplification systems proposed so far, the methods they used and discuss the strengths and shortcomings of each of them, providing direct comparison of their outputs. We aim to break some common misconceptions about what text simplification is and what it is not, and how much it has in common with text summarisation and machine translation. We believe that deeper understanding of initial motivations, and an in-depth analysis of existing TS methods would help researchers new to ATS propose even better systems, bringing fresh ideas from other related NLP areas. We will describe and explain all the most influential methods used for automatic simplification of texts so far, with the emphasis on their strengths and weaknesses noticed in a direct comparison of systems outputs. We will present all the existing resources for TS for various languages, including parallel manually produced TS corpora, comparable automatically aligned TS corpora, paraphrase- and synonym- resources, TS-specific sentence-alignment tools, and several TS evaluation resources. Finally, we will discuss the existing evaluation methodologies for TS, and necessary conditions for using each of them.

3 Tutorial Outline

- Motivation for automatic text simplification:
  - Problems for various NLP tools and applications
  - Reading difficulties of various target populations
- Text simplification projects:
  - Short description of TS projects (PSET, Simplext, PorSimples, FIRST, SIMPATICO, Able to Include)
  - Discussion about the TS projects (what they share and in what they differ)

- Text simplification resources:
  - Resources for lexical simplification
  - Resources for lexico-syntactic simplification
  - Resources for languages other than English
- Evaluation of text simplification systems:
  - Automatic evaluation
  - Human evaluation
- Comparison of non-neural text simplification approaches:
  - Rule-based systems
  - Data-driven systems (supervised and unsupervised)
  - Hybrid systems
  - Semantically-motivated ATS systems
- Neural text simplification (NTS):
  - State-of-the-art neural text simplification (NTS) systems
  - Direct comparison of NTS systems
  - Strengths and weaknesses of NTS systems

4 About the Instructors

Sanja Štajner is currently a postdoctoral research fellow at the University of Mannheim, Germany. She holds a multiple Masters degree in Natural Language Processing and Human Language Technologies (Autonomous University of Barcelona, Spain and University of Wolverhampton, UK) and the PhD degree in Computer Science from the University of Wolverhampton on the topic of "Data-driven Text Simplification". She participated in Simplext and FIRST projects on automatic text simplification, and is the lead author of four ACL papers on text simplification (including the first neural text simplification system) and numerous other papers on the topics of text simplification and readability assessment at various leading international conferences and journals. Sanja's interests in text simplification include building tools for automatic sentence alignment, building ATS systems using various approaches (machine translation, neural machine translation, event-detection, unsupervised lexical simplification), complex word identification (from eye-tracking data, and crowdsourced data), and evaluation of text simplification systems. Sanja regularly teaches NLP at Masters and PhD levels, delivers invited talks and seminars at various universities and companies, and had a very successful tutorial on Deep Learning for Text Simplification at RANLP 2017. She is an area chair for COLING 2018, and regular program committee member of ACL, EMNLP, LREC, IJCAI, IAAA and other international conferences and journals. She was a lead organizer of the first international workshop and shared task on Quality Assessment of Text Simplification (QATS) in 2016, and an organizer of Complex Word Identification shared task in 2018.

Horacio Saggion is an associate professor at the Department of Information and Communication Technologies, Universitat Pompeu Fabra, Barcelona. He is the head of the Large Scale Text Understanding Systems Lab associated to the Natural Language Processing group where he works on automatic text summarization, text simplification, information extraction, sentiment analysis and related topics. His research is empirical combining symbolic, pattern-based approaches and statistical and machine learning techniques. Before joining Universitat Pompeu Fabra as a Ramon y Cajal Fellow in 2010, he worked at the University of Sheffield for a number of UK and European research projects developing competitive human language technology. He was also an invited researcher at John Hopkins University for a project on multilingual text summarization. Horacio has been the principal investigator of several national and international projects. Horacio has published over 150 works in leading scientific journals, conferences, and books in the field of human language technology. He organized four international workshops in the areas of text summarization and information extraction and was chair of SEPLN 2014 and co-chair of STIL 2009. He is co-editor of a book on multilingual, multisource information extraction and summarization (Springer 2013) and published a book on Automatic Text Simplification (Morgan & Claypool Publishers 2017). Horacio is a member of the ACL, IEEE, ACM, and SADIO. He is a regular programme committee member for international conferences such as ACL, EACL, COLING, EMNLP, IJCNLP, IJCAI and is an active reviewer for international journals in computer science, information processing, and human language technology. Horacio has international experience in teaching and in addition to his teaching duties at UPF (and previously at Universidad de Buenos Aires) has given intensive courses, tutorials, and invited talks at a number of international events including LREC, ESSLLI, IJCNLP, NLDB, RANLP and RuSSIR.

References

Sandra Aluisio, Lucia Specia, Caroline Gasperin, and Carolina Scarton. 2010. Readability assessment for text simplification. In *Proceedings of the NAACL HLT 2010 Fifth Workshop on Innovative Use of NLP for Building Educational Applications*, pages 1–9, Stroudsburg, PA, USA. Association for Computational Linguistics.

John Carroll, Guido Minnen, Yvonne Canning, Siobhan Devlin, and John Tait. 1998. Practical simplification of English newspaper text to assist aphasic readers. In *Proceedings of the AAAI'98 Workshop on Integrating AI and Assistive Technology*, pages 7–10.

R. Chandrasekar, Christine Doran, and B. Srinivas. 1996. Motivations and methods for text simplification. In *16th International Conference on Computational Linguistics*, pages 1041–1044.

William Coster and David Kauchak. 2011. Learning to simplify sentences using Wikipedia. In *Proceedings of the Workshop on Monolingual Text-To-Text Generation*, pages 1–9, Stroudsburg, PA, USA. Association for Computational Linguistics.

Daniel Ferrés, Montserrat Marimon, Horacio Saggion, and Ahmed AbuRa'ed. 2016. YATS: Yet another text simplifier. In *Proceedings of the 21st International Conference on Applications of Natural Language to Information Systems*, pages 335–342.

William Hwang, Hannaneh Hajishirzi, Mari Ostendorf, and Wei Wu. 2015. Aligning Sentences from Standard Wikipedia to Simple Wikipedia. In *Proceedings of NAACL&HLT*, pages 211–217.

David Kauchak. 2013. Improving text simplification language modeling using unsimplified text data. In *Proceedings of the 51st Annual Meeting of the Association for Computational Linguistics*, ACL, pages 1537–1546. The Association for Computer Linguistics.

Maria Teresa Martín-Valdivia, Eugenio Martínez Cámara, Eduard Barbu, Luis Alfonso Ureña López, Paloma Moreda, and Elena Lloret. 2014. Proyecto FIRST (flexible interactive reading support tool): Desarrollo de una herramienta para ayudar a personas con autismo mediante la simplificación de textos. *Procesamiento del Lenguaje Natural*, 53:143–146.

Sergiu Nisioi, Sanja Štajner, Simone Paolo Ponzetto, and Liviu P. Dinu. 2017. Exploring neural text simplification models. In *Proceedings of the 55th Annual Meeting of the Association for Computational Linguistics (ACL)*, pages 85–91.

Gustavo H. Paetzold, Fernando Alva-Manchego, and Lucia Specia. 2017. MASSAlign: Alignment and Annotation of Comparable Documents. In *The Companion Volume of the IJCNLP 2017 Proceedings: System Demonstrations*, pages 1–4.

Ellie Pavlick and Chris Callison-Burch. 2016. Simple PPDB: A Paraphrase Database for Simplification. In *Proceedings of the 54th Annual Meeting of the Association for Computational Linguistics (Volume 2: Short Papers)*, pages 143–148. ACL.

Horacio Saggion, Sanja Štajner, Stefan Bott, Simon Mille, Luz Rello, and Biljana Drndarević. 2015. Making it Simplext: Implementation and evaluation of a text simplification system for Spanish. *ACM Transactions on Accessible Computing (TACCESS)*, 6(4):14.

Horacio Saggion, Daniel Ferrés, Leen Sevens, Ineke Schuurman, Marta Ripollés, and Olga Rodríguez. 2017. Able to read my mail: An accessible e-mail client with assistive technology. In *Proceedings of the 14th Web for All Conference on The Future of Accessible Work*, pages 5:1–5:4, New York, NY, USA. ACM.

Horacio Saggion. 2017. *Automatic Text Simplification*. Vol.32. Morgan & Claypool Publishers, first edition edition.

Horacio Saggion. 2018. Text simplification. In Ruslan Mitkov, editor, *The Oxford Handbook of Computational Linguistics (2nd edition)*, chapter 48. Oxford University Press.

Advaith Siddharthan and Angrosh Mandya. 2014. Hybrid text simplification using synchronous dependency grammars with hand-written and automatically harvested rules. In *Proceedings of the 14th Conference of the European Chapter of the Association for Computational Linguistics*, EACL, pages 722–731, Gothenburg, Sweden, April. Association for Computational Linguistics.

Advaith Siddharthan. 2006. Syntactic simplification and text cohesion. *Research on Language and Computation*, 4(1):77–109.

Lucia Specia. 2010. Translating from complex to simplified sentences. In *Proceedings of the 9th International Conference on Computational Processing of the Portuguese Language*, PROPOR, pages 30–39, Porto Alegre, RS, Brazil, April 27-30.

Sanja Štajner and Sergiu Nisioi. 2018. A Detailed Evaluation of Neural Sequence-to-Sequence Models for In-domain and Cross-domain Text Simplification. In *Proceedings of the Eleventh International Conference on Language Resources and Evaluation (LREC 2018)*, Miyazaki, Japan, May 7-12, 2018. European Language Resources Association (ELRA).

Sanja Štajner, Marc Franco-Salvador, Simone Paolo Ponzetto, Paolo Rosso, and Heiner Stuckenschmidt. 2017. Sentence alignment methods for improving text simplification systems. In *Proceedings of the 55th Annual Meeting of the Association for Computational Linguistics (ACL)*, pages 97–102.

Sanja Štajner, Marc Franco-Salvador, Paolo Rosso, and Simone Paolo Ponzetto. 2018. CATS: A Tool for Customized Alignment of Text Simplification Corpora. In *Proceedings of the Eleventh International Conference on Language Resources and Evaluation (LREC 2018)*, Miyazaki, Japan, May 7-12, 2018. European Language Resources Association (ELRA).

Wei Xu, Chris Callison-Burch, and Courtney Napoles. 2015. Problems in current text simplification research: New data can help. *Transactions of the Associaton for Computational Linguistics*, 3:283–297.

Wei Xu, Courtney Napoles, Ellie Pavlick, Quanze Chen, and Chris Callison-Burch. 2016. Optimizing statistical machine translation for text simplification. *Transactions of the Association for Computational Linguistics*, 4:401–415.

Xingxing Zhang and Mirella Lapata. 2017. Sentence Simplification with Deep Reinforcement Learning. In *Proceedings of the 2017 Conference on Empirical Methods in Natural Language Processing*, pages 584–594.

Zhemin Zhu, Delphine Bernhard, and Iryna Gurevych. 2010. A monolingual tree-based translation model for sentence simplification. In *Proceedings of the 23rd International Conference on Computational Linguistics*, COLING, pages 1353–1361, Beijing, China, August.

Deep Learning for Dialogue Systems

Yun-Nung Chen
National Taiwan University
Taipei, Taiwan
y.v.chen@ieee.org

Asli Celikyilmaz
Microsoft Research
Redmond, WA
asli@ieee.org

Dilek Hakkani-Tür
Google Research
Mountain View, CA
dilek@ieee.org

Abstract

Goal-oriented spoken dialogue systems have been the most prominent component in todays virtual personal assistants, which allow users to speak naturally in order to finish tasks more efficiently. The advancement of deep learning technologies has recently risen the applications of neural models to dialogue modeling. However, applying deep learning technologies for building robust and scalable dialogue systems is still a challenging task and an open research area as it requires deeper understanding of the classic pipelines as well as detailed knowledge of the prior work and the recent state-of-the-art work. Therefore, this tutorial is designed to focus on an overview of dialogue system development while describing most recent research for building dialogue systems, and summarizing the challenges, in order to allow researchers to study the potential improvements of the state-of-the-art dialogue systems. The tutorial material is available at http://deepdialogue.miulab.tw.

1 Tutorial Overview

With the rising trend of artificial intelligence, more and more devices have incorporated goal-oriented spoken dialogue systems. Among popular virtual personal assistants, Microsoft's Cortana, Apple's Siri, Amazon Alexa, and Google Assistant have incorporated dialogue system modules in various devices, which allow users to speak naturally in order to finish tasks more efficiently.

Traditional conversational systems have rather complex and/or modular pipelines. The advancement of deep learning technologies has recently risen the applications of neural models to dialogue modeling. Nevertheless, applying deep learning technologies for building robust and scalable dialogue systems is still a challenging task and an open research area as it requires deeper understanding of the classic pipelines as well as detailed knowledge on the benchmark of the models of the prior work and the recent state-of-the-art work.

The goal of this tutorial is to provide the audience with the developing trend of dialogue systems, and a roadmap to get them started with the related work. The first section motivates the work on conversation-based intelligent agents, in which the core underlying system is task-oriented dialogue systems. The following section describes different approaches using deep learning for each component in the dialogue system and how it is evaluated. The last two sections focus on discussing the recent trends and current challenges on dialogue system technology and summarize the challenges and conclusions. The detailed content is described as follows.

2 Dialogue System Basics

This section will motivate the work on conversation-based intelligent agents, in which the core underlying system is task-oriented spoken dialogue systems.

The section starts with an overview of the standard pipeline framework for dialogue system illustrated in Figure 1 (Tur and De Mori, 2011). Basic components of a dialog system are automatic speech recognition (ASR), language understanding (LU), dialogue management (DM), and natural language generation (NLG) (Rudnicky et al., 1999; Zue et al., 2000; Zue and Glass, 2000). This tutorial will mainly focus on LU, DM, and NLG parts.

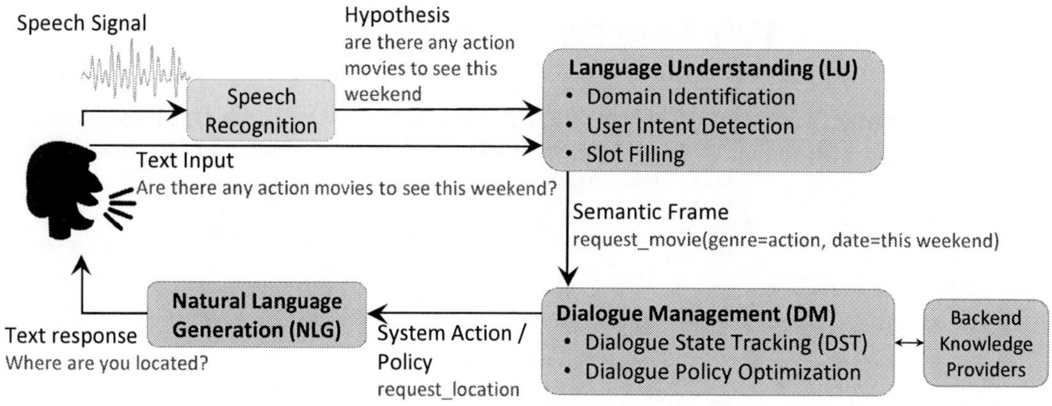

Figure 1: Pipeline framework of spoken dialog system.

Language Understanding Traditionally, domain identification and intent prediction are framed as utterance classification problems, where several classifiers such as support vector machines and maximum entropy have been employed (Haffner et al., 2003; Chelba et al., 2003; Chen et al., 2014). Then slot filling is framed as a word sequence tagging task, where the IOB (in-out-begin) format is applied for representing slot tags, and hidden Markov models (HMM) or conditional random fields (CRF) have been employed for slot tagging (Pieraccini et al., 1992; Wang et al., 2005; Raymond and Riccardi, 2007).

Dialogue Management A partially observable Markov decision process (POMDP) has been shown to be beneficial by allowing the dialogue manager to be optimized to plan and act under the uncertainty created by noisy speech recognition and semantic decoding (Williams and Young, 2007; Young et al., 2013). The POMDP policy controlling the actions taken by the system is trained in an episodic reinforcement learning (RL) framework whereby the agent receives a reinforcement signal after each dialogue (episode) reflecting how well it performed (Sutton and Barto, 1998). In addition, the dialogue states should be tracked in order to measure the belief of the current situation during the whole interaction (Young et al., 2010; Sun et al., 2014).

Natural Language Generation There are two NLG approaches, one focuses on generating text using templates or rules (linguistic) methods, the another uses corpus-based statistical techniques (Oh and Rudnicky, 2002). Oh and Rudnicky showed that stochastic generation benefits from two factors: 1) it takes advantage of the practical language of a domain expert instead of the developer and 2) it restates the problem in terms of classification and labeling, where expertise is not required for developing a rule-based generation system.

3 Deep Learning Based Dialogue System

With the power of deep learning, there is increasing research work focusing on applying deep learning for each component.

Language Understanding With the advances on deep learning, neural models have been applied to domain and intent classification tasks (Sarikaya et al., 2011; Tur et al., 2012; Sarikaya et al., 2014). Ravuri and Stolcke (2015) first proposed an RNN architecture for intent determination. For slot filling, deep learning has been viewed as a feature generator and the neural architecture can be merged with CRFs (Xu and Sarikaya, 2013). Yao et al. (2013) and Mesnil et al. (2015) later employed RNNs for sequence labeling in order to perform slot filling. Such architectures have later been extended to jointly model intent detection and slot filling in multiple domains (Hakkani-Tür et al., 2016; Jaech et al., 2016). Recently, Zhai et al. (2017) proposed to tag the semantic labels together with segmentation and achieved the state-of-the-art performance.

In addition, how to leverage contextual information and prior linguistic knowledge performs better understanding is an important issue. End-to-end memory networks have been shown to provide a good mechanism for integrating longer term knowledge context and shorter term dialogue context into these models (Chen et al., 2016b; Chen et al., 2016c). In addition, the importance of the LU module is investigated in Li et al. (2017a), where different types of errors from LU may degrade the whole system performance in an reinforcement learning setting.

Dialogue Management – Dialogue State Tracking The state-of-the-art dialogue managers focus on monitoring the dialogue progress by neural dialogue state trackers. Among the initial models are the RNN based dialogue state tracking approaches (Henderson et al., 2013) that has shown to outperform Bayesian networks (Thomson and Young, 2010). More recent work that provided conjoint representations between the utterances, slot-value pairs as well as knowledge graph representations (Wen et al., 2016; Mrkšić et al., 2016) demonstrated that using neural dialogue models can overcome current obstacles of deploying dialogue systems in larger dialogue domains. Rastogi et al. (2017) also proposed a multi-domain dialogue state tracker to achieve effective and efficient domain adaptation.

Dialogue Management – Dialogue Policy Optimization The dialogue policy can be learned in either a supervised or a reinforcement learning manner (Su et al., 2016). The reinforcement learning based dialogue agent has been recently developed in different tasks and shown applicable for interactive scenarios (Li et al., 2017b; Dhingra et al., 2017; Shah et al., 2016). In order to enable reinforcement learning, a simulated environment is required. Several approaches are proposed for building user simulators as the interactive environment (Li et al., 2016; El Asri et al., 2016; Crook and Marin, 2017), so that the dialogue policy can be trained in a reinforcement framework.

Natural Language Generation The RNN-based models have been applied to language generation for both chit-chat and task-orientated dialogue systems (Vinyals and Le, 2015; Wen et al., 2015b). The RNN-based NLG can learn from unaligned data by jointly optimizing sentence planning and surface realization, and language variation can be easily achieved by sampling from output candidates (Wen et al., 2015a). Moreover, Wen et al. (2015b) improved the prior work by adding a gating mechanism for controlling the dialogue act during generation in order to avoid semantics repetition, showing promising results. Several aspects of improvement have been achieved using contextual and structured information (Dušek and Jurcicek, 2016; Nayak et al., 2017; Su et al., 2018)

4 Recent Trends and Challenges on Learning Dialogues

This part will focus on discussing the recent trends and current challenges on dialogue system technology.

End-to-End Learning for Dialogue Systems With the power of neural networks, there are more and more attempts for learning dialogue systems in an end-to-end fashion. Different learning frameworks are applied, including supervised learning and reinforcement learning. This part will discuss the work about end-to-end learning for dialogues (Dhingra et al., 2016; Wen et al., 2016; Williams and Zweig, 2016; Zhao and Eskenazi, 2016; Li et al., 2017b).

Recent advance of deep learning has inspired many applications of neural models to dialogue systems. Wen et al. (2016) and Bordes and Weston (2016) introduced a network-based end-to-end trainable task-oriented dialogue system, which treated dialogue system learning as the problem of learning a mapping from dialogue histories to system responses, and applied an encoder-decoder model to train the whole system. However, the system is trained in a supervised fashion, thus requires a lot of training data, and may not be able to explore the unknown space that does not exist in the training data for an optimal and robust policy.

Zhao and Eskenazi (2016) first presented an end-to-end reinforcement learning (RL) approach to dialogue state tracking and policy learning in the DM. This approach is shown to be promising when applied to a task-oriented system, which is to guess the famous person a user thinks of. In the conversation, the agent asks the user a series of Yes/No questions to find the correct answer. Dhingra et al. (2016) proposed an end-to-end differentiable KB-Infobot to improve the flexibility of question types and robustness. Li et al. (2017b) further presented an end-to-end neural dialogue system for completing tasks, which supported flexible question types, allowed user-initiated requests during conversation, and finally achieved better robustness. Human feedback is also effectively leveraged into the learning framework for on-line training in an end-to-end manner (Liu et al., 2018).

Dialogue Breadth In order to extend the coverage of the systems, transfer learning has been applied to different extended systems in order to proceed to a multi-domain scenario. Chen et al. (2016a) transfered the dialogue acts across different domains so that the performance of the newly-developed domain can be boosted. Kim et al. (2016) proposed to learn a domain-specific and domain-independent information in order to transfer the shared knowledge more efficiently and effectively. In addition, Gašić et al. (2015) presented the policy committee in order to boost the performance for policy training in a new domain. All above work extended the dialogue coverage using different directions.

Dialogue Depth Most current systems focus on knowledge-based understanding, but there are hierarchical understanding according to the dialogue complexity. For example, an intent about party scheduling may include restaurant reserving and invitation sending. Sun et al. (2016) learned the high-level intentions that span on multiple domains in order to achieve common sense understanding. Moreover, a more complex dialogue such as "*I feel sad...*" requires empathy in order to generate the suitable response. Fung et al. (2016) first attempted to leverage different modalities for emotion detection and built an emotion-aware dialogue system.

Given two branches of development, the ultimate goal is to build an open-domain dialogue system (coverage) with all levels of understanding (depth).

5 Tutorial Instructors

Yun-Nung (Vivian) Chen is an assistant professor in the Department of Computer Science and Information Engineering at National Taiwan University. Her research interests focus on spoken dialogue system, language understanding, natural language processing, deep learning, and multimodality. She received Google Faulty Research Awards 2016, MOST Young Scholar Fellowship 2018, NVIDIA 2017 Best Scientific Research Award, two Best Student Paper Awards from IEEE ASRU 2013 and IEEE SLT 2010 and a Student Best Paper Nominee from INTERSPEECH 2012. Chen earned the Ph.D. degree from School of Computer Science at Carnegie Mellon University, Pittsburgh in 2015. Prior to joining National Taiwan University, she worked in the Deep Learning Technology Center at Microsoft Research, Redmond.

- Affiliation: National Taiwan University, Taipei, Taiwan
- Email: `y.v.chen@ieee.org`
- Website: `http://vivianchen.idv.tw`

Asli Celikyilmaz is currently a researcher at the Deep Learning Technology Center at Microsfot Research. Previously, she was a Research Scientist at Microsoft Bing from 2010 until 2016 focusing on deep learning models for scaling natural user interfaces to multiple domains. She has worked as a Postdoc Researcher at the EECS Department of the UC Berkeley from 2008 until 2010. She has worked with researchers at ICSI @ Berkeley during her postdoc research study. She has earned her Ph.D. from University of Toronto, Canada in 2008. Asli's research interests are mainly machine learning and its applications to conversational dialogue systems, mainly natural language understanding and dialogue modeling. In the past she has also focused on research areas including machine intelligence, semantic tagging of natural user utterances of human to machine conversations, text analysis, document summarization, question answering, co-reference resolution, to name a few. Currently she is focusing on reasoning, attention, memory networks as well as multi-task and transfer learning for conversational dialogue systems. She has been serving as area chair, co-organizer of numerous NLP and speech conferences, such as ACL, NAACL, Interspeech, and IEEE Spoken Language Technologies (SLT). She co-organized a NIPS workshop on Machine Learning for Spoken Language Understanding and Interactions in 2015.

- Affiliation: Microsoft Research, Redmond, WA
- Email: `asli@ieee.org`

- Website: http://www.microsoft.com/en-us/research/people/aslicel

Dilek Hakkani-Tür is a research scientist at Google Research. Prior to joining Google, she was a researcher at Microsoft Research (2010-2016), International Computer Science Institute (ICSI, 2006-2010) and AT&T Labs-Research (2001-2005). She received her BSc degree from Middle East Technical Univ, in 1994, and MSc and PhD degrees from Bilkent Univ., Department of Computer Engineering, in 1996 and 2000, respectively. Her research interests include natural language and speech processing, spoken dialogue systems, and machine learning for language processing. She has over 50 patents that were granted and co-authored more than 200 papers in natural language and speech processing. She is the recipient of three best paper awards for her work on active learning for dialogue systems, from IEEE Signal Processing Society, ISCA and EURASIP. She was an associate editor of IEEE Transactions on Audio, Speech and Language Processing (2005-2008), member of the IEEE Speech and Language Technical Committee (2009-2014), area editor for speech and language processing for Elsevier's Digital Signal Processing Journal and IEEE Signal Processing Letters (2011-2013). She currently serves on the ISCA Advisory Council (2015-2018) and as the editor-in-chief of the IEEE/ACM Transactions on Audio, Speech and Language Processing. She is a fellow of IEEE and ISCA.

- Affiliation: Google Research, Mountain View, CA
- Email: dilek@ieee.org
- Website: https://ai.google/research/people/104927

References

Antoine Bordes and Jason Weston. 2016. Learning end-to-end goal-oriented dialog. *arXiv preprint arXiv:1605.07683.*

Ciprian Chelba, Monika Mahajan, and Alex Acero. 2003. Speech utterance classification. In *2003 IEEE International Conference on Acoustics, Speech, and Signal Processing, 2003. Proceedings.(ICASSP)*, volume 1, pages I–280. IEEE.

Yun-Nung Chen, Dilek Hakkani-Tur, and Gokan Tur. 2014. Deriving local relational surface forms from dependency-based entity embeddings for unsupervised spoken language understanding. In *2014 IEEE Spoken Language Technology Workshop (SLT)*, pages 242–247. IEEE.

Yun-Nung Chen, Dilek Hakkani-T, Xiaodong He, et al. 2016a. Zero-shot learning of intent embeddings for expansion by convolutional deep structured semantic models. In *2016 IEEE International Conference on Acoustics, Speech and Signal Processing (ICASSP)*, pages 6045–6049. IEEE.

Yun-Nung Chen, Dilek Hakkani-Tur, Gokhan Tur, Asli Celikyilmaz, Jianfeng Gao, and Li Deng. 2016b. Knowledge as a teacher: Knowledge-guided structural attention networks. *arXiv preprint arXiv:1609.03286.*

Yun-Nung Chen, Dilek Hakkani-Tür, Gokhan Tur, Jianfeng Gao, and Li Deng. 2016c. End-to-end memory networks with knowledge carryover for multi-turn spoken language understanding. In *Proceedings of the Interspeech.*

Paul Crook and Alex Marin. 2017. Sequence to sequence modeling for user simulation in dialog systems. In *Proceedings of INTERSPEECH*, pages 1706–1710.

Bhuwan Dhingra, Lihong Li, Xiujun Li, Jianfeng Gao, Yun-Nung Chen, Faisal Ahmed, and Li Deng. 2016. End-to-end reinforcement learning of dialogue agents for information access. *arXiv preprint arXiv:1609.00777.*

Bhuwan Dhingra, Lihong Li, Xiujun Li, Jianfeng Gao, Yun-Nung Chen, Faisal Ahmed, and Li Deng. 2017. Towards end-to-end reinforcement learning of dialogue agents for information access. In *Proceedings of ACL*, pages 484–495.

Ondřej Dušek and Filip Jurcicek. 2016. A context-aware natural language generator for dialogue systems. In *Proceedings of SIGDIAL*, pages 185–190.

Layla El Asri, Jing He, and Kaheer Suleman. 2016. A sequence-to-sequence model for user simulation in spoken dialogue systems. In *Proceedings of INTERSPEECH.*

Pascale Fung, Dario Bertero, Yan Wan, Anik Dey, Ricky Ho Yin Chan, Farhad Bin Siddique, Yang Yang, Chien-Sheng Wu, and Ruixi Lin. 2016. Towards empathetic human-robot interactions. *arXiv preprint arXiv:1605.04072.*

M Gašić, N Mrkšić, Pei-hao Su, David Vandyke, Tsung-Hsien Wen, and Steve Young. 2015. Policy committee for adaptation in multi-domain spoken dialogue systems. In *Automatic Speech Recognition and Understanding (ASRU), 2015 IEEE Workshop on*, pages 806–812. IEEE.

Patrick Haffner, Gokhan Tur, and Jerry H Wright. 2003. Optimizing svms for complex call classification. In *2003 IEEE International Conference on Acoustics, Speech, and Signal Processing, 2003. Proceedings.(ICASSP)*, volume 1, pages I–632. IEEE.

Dilek Hakkani-Tür, Gokhan Tur, Asli Celikyilmaz, Yun-Nung Chen, Jianfeng Gao, Li Deng, and Ye-Yi Wang. 2016. Multi-domain joint semantic frame parsing using bi-directional RNN-LSTM. In *Proceedings of the Interspeech*, San Francisco, CA.

Matthew Henderson, Blaise Thomson, and Steve Young. 2013. Deep neural network approach for the dialog state tracking challenge. In *Proceedings of the SIGDIAL 2013 Conference*, pages 467–471.

A. Jaech, L. Heck, and M. Ostendorf. 2016. Domain adaptation of recurrent neural networks for natural language understanding. In *Proceedings of the Interspeech*, San Francisco, CA.

Young-Bum Kim, Karl Stratos, and Ruhi Sarikaya. 2016. Frustratingly easy neural domain adaptation. In *Proceedings of COLING*, pages 387–396.

Xiujun Li, Zachary C Lipton, Bhuwan Dhingra, Lihong Li, Jianfeng Gao, and Yun-Nung Chen. 2016. A user simulator for task-completion dialogues. *arXiv preprint arXiv:1612.05688*.

Xiujun Li, Yun-Nung Chen, Lihong Li, Jianfeng Gao, and Asli Celikyilmaz. 2017a. Investigation of language understanding impact for reinforcement learning based dialogue systems. *arXiv preprint arXiv:1703.07055*.

Xuijun Li, Yun-Nung Chen, Lihong Li, Jianfeng Gao, and Asli Celikyilmaz. 2017b. End-to-end task-completion neural dialogue systems. In *Proceedings of IJCNLP*.

Bing Liu, Gokhan Tür, Dilek Hakkani-Tür, Pararth Shah, and Larry Heck. 2018. Dialogue learning with human teaching and feedback in end-to-end trainable task-oriented dialogue systems. In *Proceedings of NAACL-HLT*, pages 2060–2069.

Grégoire Mesnil, Yann Dauphin, Kaisheng Yao, Yoshua Bengio, Li Deng, Dilek Hakkani-Tur, Xiaodong He, Larry Heck, Gokhan Tur, Dong Yu, et al. 2015. Using recurrent neural networks for slot filling in spoken language understanding. *IEEE/ACM Transactions on Audio, Speech, and Language Processing*, 23(3):530–539.

Nikola Mrkšić, Diarmuid Ó Séaghdha, Tsung-Hsien Wen, Blaise Thomson, and Steve Young. 2016. Neural belief tracker: Data-driven dialogue state tracking. *arXiv preprint arXiv:1606.03777*.

Neha Nayak, Dilek Hakkani-Tur, Marilyn Walker, and Larry Heck. 2017. To plan or not to plan? discourse planning in slot-value informed sequence to sequence models for language generation. In *Proceedings of Interspeech*.

Alice H Oh and Alexander I Rudnicky. 2002. Stochastic natural language generation for spoken dialog systems. *Computer Speech & Language*, 16(3):387–407.

Roberto Pieraccini, Evelyne Tzoukermann, Zakhar Gorelov, Jean-Luc Gauvain, Esther Levin, Chin-Hui Lee, and Jay G Wilpon. 1992. A speech understanding system based on statistical representation of semantics. In *1992 IEEE International Conference on Acoustics, Speech, and Signal Processing (ICASSP)*, volume 1, pages 193–196. IEEE.

Abhinav Rastogi, Dilek Hakkani-Tur, and Larry Heck. 2017. Scalable multi-domain dialogue state tracking. In *Proceedings of ASRU*.

Suman Ravuri and Andreas Stolcke. 2015. Recurrent neural network and LSTM models for lexical utterance classification. In *Sixteenth Annual Conference of the International Speech Communication Association*.

Christian Raymond and Giuseppe Riccardi. 2007. Generative and discriminative algorithms for spoken language understanding. In *INTERSPEECH*, pages 1605–1608.

Alexander I Rudnicky, Eric H Thayer, Paul C Constantinides, Chris Tchou, R Shern, Kevin A Lenzo, Wei Xu, and Alice Oh. 1999. Creating natural dialogs in the carnegie mellon communicator system. In *Eurospeech*.

Ruhi Sarikaya, Geoffrey E Hinton, and Bhuvana Ramabhadran. 2011. Deep belief nets for natural language call-routing. In *2011 IEEE International Conference on Acoustics, Speech and Signal Processing (ICASSP)*, pages 5680–5683. IEEE.

Ruhi Sarikaya, Geoffrey E Hinton, and Anoop Deoras. 2014. Application of deep belief networks for natural language understanding. *IEEE/ACM Transactions on Audio, Speech, and Language Processing*, 22(4):778–784.

Pararth Shah, Dilek Hakkani-Tur, and Larry Heck. 2016. Interactive reinforcement learning for task-oriented dialogue management. In *Proceedings of NIPS 2016 Workshop on Deep Learning for Action and Interaction*.

Pei-Hao Su, Milica Gasic, Nikola Mrksic, Lina Rojas-Barahona, Stefan Ultes, David Vandyke, Tsung-Hsien Wen, and Steve Young. 2016. On-line active reward learning for policy optimisation in spoken dialogue systems. *arXiv preprint arXiv:1605.07669*.

Shang-Yu Su, Kai-Ling Lo, Yi Ting Yeh, and Yun-Nung Chen. 2018. Natural language generation by hierarchical decoding with linguistic patterns. In *Proceedings of NAACL-HLT*, pages 61–66.

Kai Sun, Lu Chen, Su Zhu, and Kai Yu. 2014. A generalized rule based tracker for dialogue state tracking. In *Spoken Language Technology Workshop (SLT), 2014 IEEE*, pages 330–335. IEEE.

Ming Sun, Yun-Nung Chen, and Alexander I Rudnicky. 2016. An intelligent assistant for high-level task understanding. In *Proceedings of the 21st International Conference on Intelligent User Interfaces*, pages 169–174. ACM.

Richard S Sutton and Andrew G Barto. 1998. *Reinforcement learning: An introduction*, volume 1. MIT press Cambridge.

Blaise Thomson and Steve Young. 2010. Bayesian update of dialogue state: A POMDP framework for spoken dialogue systems. *Computer Speech and Language*, 24(4):562–588.

Gokhan Tur and Renato De Mori. 2011. *Spoken language understanding: Systems for extracting semantic information from speech*. John Wiley & Sons.

Gokhan Tur, Li Deng, Dilek Hakkani-Tür, and Xiaodong He. 2012. Towards deeper understanding: Deep convex networks for semantic utterance classification. In *2012 IEEE International Conference on Acoustics, Speech and Signal Processing (ICASSP)*, pages 5045–5048. IEEE.

Oriol Vinyals and Quoc Le. 2015. A neural conversational model. *arXiv preprint arXiv:1506.05869*.

Ye-Yi Wang, Li Deng, and Alex Acero. 2005. Spoken language understanding. *IEEE Signal Processing Magazine*, 22(5):16–31.

Tsung-Hsien Wen, Milica Gašic, Dongho Kim, Nikola Mrkšic, Pei-Hao Su, David Vandyke, and Steve Young. 2015a. Stochastic language generation in dialogue using recurrent neural networks with convolutional sentence reranking. In *16th Annual Meeting of the Special Interest Group on Discourse and Dialogue*, page 275.

Tsung-Hsien Wen, Milica Gasic, Nikola Mrksic, Pei-Hao Su, David Vandyke, and Steve Young. 2015b. Semantically conditioned lstm-based natural language generation for spoken dialogue systems. *arXiv preprint arXiv:1508.01745*.

Tsung-Hsien Wen, Milica Gasic, Nikola Mrksic, Lina M Rojas-Barahona, Pei-Hao Su, Stefan Ultes, David Vandyke, and Steve Young. 2016. A network-based end-to-end trainable task-oriented dialogue system. *arXiv preprint arXiv:1604.04562*.

Jason D Williams and Steve Young. 2007. Partially observable markov decision processes for spoken dialog systems. *Computer Speech & Language*, 21(2):393–422.

Jason D Williams and Geoffrey Zweig. 2016. End-to-end LSTM-based dialog control optimized with supervised and reinforcement learning. *arXiv preprint arXiv:1606.01269*.

Puyang Xu and Ruhi Sarikaya. 2013. Convolutional neural network based triangular CRF for joint intent detection and slot filling. In *2013 IEEE Workshop on Automatic Speech Recognition and Understanding (ASRU)*, pages 78–83. IEEE.

Kaisheng Yao, Geoffrey Zweig, Mei-Yuh Hwang, Yangyang Shi, and Dong Yu. 2013. Recurrent neural networks for language understanding. In *INTERSPEECH*, pages 2524–2528.

Steve Young, Milica Gašić, Simon Keizer, François Mairesse, Jost Schatzmann, Blaise Thomson, and Kai Yu. 2010. The hidden information state model: A practical framework for pomdp-based spoken dialogue management. *Computer Speech & Language*, 24(2):150–174.

Steve Young, Milica Gašić, Blaise Thomson, and Jason D Williams. 2013. POMDP-based statistical spoken dialog systems: A review. *Proceedings of the IEEE*, 101(5):1160–1179.

Feifei Zhai, Saloni Potdar, Bing Xiang, and Bowen Zhou. 2017. Neural models for sequence chunking. In *Proceedings of AAAI*, pages 3365–3371.

Tiancheng Zhao and Maxine Eskenazi. 2016. Towards end-to-end learning for dialog state tracking and management using deep reinforcement learning. *arXiv preprint arXiv:1606.02560*.

Victor W Zue and James R Glass. 2000. Conversational interfaces: Advances and challenges. *Proceedings of the IEEE*, 88(8):1166–1180.

Victor Zue, Stephanie Seneff, James R Glass, Joseph Polifroni, Christine Pao, Timothy J Hazen, and Lee Hetherington. 2000. JUPITER: a telephone-based conversational interface for weather information. *IEEE Transactions on speech and audio processing*, 8(1):85–96.

Association for Computational Linguistics
209 N. Eighth Street
Stroudsburg, Pennsylvania 18360

ISBN 978-1-5108-6906-6

CURRAN ASSOCIATES INC.
proceedings.com